REPTILES & AMPHIBIANS

Written by Joanne Mattern

Photographs by Lynn M. Stone

Watermill Press

Frogs are part of a group of animals called amphibians (am-FIB-ee-uns). Most amphibians have smooth, damp skin. They live part of their lives in the water, and part of their lives on land.

This toad's body is drier and bumpier than a frog's. But in many ways toads and frogs are alike. Many toads and frogs can puff out their throats and make a loud croaking noise. This is how they "talk" to one another.

A newt is a small amphibian. Newts lay their eggs on plants that grow underwater. When the babies hatch, they live in the water until they grow lungs. Then the newts move onto the land. They often live under fallen leaves, where it is damp and cool.

Snakes belong to a group of animals called reptiles. Reptiles and amphibians are alike in some ways. But instead of having smooth, damp skin, a reptile is covered with dry scales. Most reptiles spend almost all their lives on land.

The rattlesnake got its name because the hard, dry scales at the end of its tail sound like a rattle when it moves. Most snakes are not harmful to people, but a rattlesnake's bite is poisonous.

Can you find a horned lizard hiding in this picture? It is hard to see because the lizard is the same color as the rocks around it. This helps the horned lizard hide from other animals. Horned lizards are reptiles. They live in the desert, where it is very hot and dry.

A turtle is the only reptile that has a shell. A turtle's shell can be many different colors. It can even have stripes or spots! These patterns make the turtle hard to see as it rests on grass or fallen leaves.

A turtle moves slowly, so it cannot run away from an enemy. Instead, most turtles protect themselves by pulling their head, legs, and tail into their shell. There it is safe from almost any danger.

The loggerhead sea turtle buries her eggs in the sand where they will be safe and warm. Then she returns to the sea. When the eggs hatch, the tiny babies will crawl to the water and swim away. They will spend almost all their lives in the ocean.

Alligators are very large reptiles. They usually walk slowly on land, because their legs are short. But an alligator can swim quickly. It glides through the water with only its eyes and nose showing, looking for fish, turtles, and other animals to eat.

This is a crocodile. Crocodiles and alligators look a lot alike. But there are ways to tell them apart. An alligator's jaw is rounded, but a crocodile's is pointed. And a crocodile's front teeth stick out even when its mouth is closed!

Index

LIBRARY OF CONGRESS CATALOGING-IN-PUBLICATION DATA
Mattern, Joanne, (date)
    Reptiles and amphibians / by Joanne Mattern; photographs by Lynn
M. Stone.
      p.   cm.
    Summary: Describes the characteristics of various reptiles and
amphibians, including the frog, snake, and crocodile.
    ISBN 0-8167-2954-9 (pbk.)
    1. Reptiles—Juvenile literature.   2. Amphibians—Juvenile
literature. [1. Reptiles. 2. Amphibians.] I. Stone, Lynn M.,
ill. II. Title.
QL644.2.M316   1993
597.9—dc20   92-20189

Photo credits:
Photographs © 1993 by Lynn M. Stone   Cover photo © 1993 by Lynn M. Stone